UNDERSTAND

RAP

EXPLANATIONS OF
CONFUSING RAP LYRICS
YOU & YOUR GRANDMA
CAN UNDERSTAND

WILLIAM BUCKHOLZ

ABRAMS IMAGE, NEW YORK

Cataloging-in-Publication Data has been applied for and
may be obtained from the Library of Congress.
ISBN 978-0-8109-8921-4

Printed and bound in U.S.A.
20 19 18 17

Abrams Image books are available at special discounts when purchased in quantity
for premiums and promotions as well as fundraising or educational use.
Special editions can also be created to specification.
For details, contact specialsales@abramsbooks.com, or the address below.

THE ART OF BOOKS SINCE 1949

115 West 18th Street
New York, NY 10011
www.abramsbooks.com

This book is dedicated to Mom and Dad for always encouraging me, and my brother, Tom, for renewing my interest in rap music.

CONTENTS

AUTHOR'S NOTE

UNDERSTAND RAP is a work of music scholarship that attempts to creatively translate interesting and confusing rap lyrics into language those unfamiliar with rap culture and slang can understand.

While at times humorous because of the contrast between the artists' language and the language of the author, the intention of this book is not to poke fun at rap music. Rather, it is to highlight some of the more creative artists and lyrics in the genre today and to bring a basic understanding of concepts and themes in rap music to the attention of an audience who may not otherwise be exposed to these lyrics or give them a second thought. It is not the intention of the author to glorify drug use, violence, crime, or sexual promiscuity, even if such themes or concepts are analyzed in this book. It should also be noted that guests often appear on other artists' albums and therefore the artist or artists listed beneath a lyric may not be the artist who authored or recited the lyric. Each explanation presented for a lyric in this book represents one of many possible interpretations of these musical works of art, and they are not meant to be taken as fact or to represent the artists' points of view in any way whatsoever. Any inaccuracies in the lyrics are unintentional. If used or implied, the first person point of view does not necessarily reflect the views of the artist and is used purely for illustrative purposes. Please support all the artists referenced in this book by purchasing and listening to their albums.

MONEY

GOT SO MUCH CHIPS, I SWEAR THEY CALL ME HEWLETT-PACKARD

LYRIC FROM SONG: **"LOLLIPOP (REMIX)"**   ON ALBUM: **THA CARTER III (ITUNES BONUS TRACK)** BY ARTIST: **LIL WAYNE**

I am so wealthy that people might mistakenly refer to me by the name of a large multinational computer manufacturer whose integrated circuits are commonly referred to by the same name that I and others use for money.

I GOT RUBBER BAND BANKS IN MY POCKET

LYRIC FROM SONG: **"WHATEVER YOU LIKE"**   ON ALBUM: **PAPER TRAIL**   BY ARTIST: **T.I.**

I carry such large amounts of cash around with me that a wallet would quickly wear out as it would be stretched beyond the capacity to hold the currency for which it was designed. A common alternative to the wallet, the money clip, is pushed beyond its mechanical limit as well. Therefore, a large rubber band will be employed, as it can expand with increased capacity.

IT AIN'T MY BIRTHDAY BUT I GOT MY NAME ON THE CAKE

LYRIC FROM SONG: **"STUNTIN' LIKE MY DADDY"** ON ALBUM: **LIKE FATHER, LIKE SON** BY ARTIST: **BIRDMAN AND LIL WAYNE**

One of the names for money is the same as the dessert that is eaten in celebration of another year a human has lived. While no one would observe an annually occurring day 365 times a year, each day is equally joyous to me because of the income that is constantly flowing in, and is therefore worthy of celebration.

AFTER BIG BUCKS, NO WHAMMY

LYRIC FROM SONG: **"WEED & MONEY"** ON ALBUM: **GHETTO D** BY ARTIST: **MASTER P**

There are some risks when it comes to the pursuit of financial success in the rap industry, just as contestants on 1980s television game show *Press Your Luck* risked losing all their money at the hands of a creepy red cartoon character.

SWIMMING IN THE MONEY, COME AND FIND ME, NEMO

LYRIC FROM SONG: **"FOREVER"** BY ARTIST: **DRAKE**
ON ALBUM: **MORE THAN A GAME (SOUNDTRACK)**

It is possible that you could have so much money that there would be nowhere practical to store it all and eventually every room of your house would be filled with paper currency. Anyone who stopped by to visit you in this virtual ocean of money would have as much trouble finding you as an animated talking cartoon fish father had finding his animated talking cartoon fish son.

YOU ON THE INTERNET PRICING

LYRIC FROM SONG: **"HE TRIED TO PLAY ME"**   ON ALBUM: **KILLA SEASON**
BY ARTIST: **CAM'RON**

It is funny that you are using a vast network of computers in order
to find the most affordable items as you research bargains and
compare the costs associated with shopping at various stores,
while other people simply purchase whatever they want immediately upon seeing it and without regard for cost.

IT'S A BLESSIN' TO BLOW A HUNDRED THOU' IN A RECESSION

LYRIC FROM SONG: **"KINDA LIKE A BIG DEAL"**   ON ALBUM: **TIL THE CASKET DROPS**
BY ARTIST: **CLIPSE**

One must believe God is looking favorably upon oneself to be able to frivolously spend $100,000 without worrying about how their bank account balance will be affected during a time when most of the population is struggling financially due to an economic crisis.

USED TO MAKE A THOUSAND DOLLARS EVERY TIME I PLAYED HOOKY

LYRIC FROM SONG: **"FEEL ME"**   ON ALBUM: **THA CARTER II**   BY ARTIST: **LIL WAYNE**

It is possible that while skipping school, rather than going to the mall, watching a movie, or socializing with friends, one could be engaging in lucrative activities, such as drug dealing, that might yield amounts of money much greater than the average student's allowance or summer job.

GRINDIN' DAILY TO STACK MY BREAD

LYRIC FROM SONG: **"THEY DON'T KNOW"**   ON ALBUM: **THE PEOPLES CHAMP**
BY ARTIST: **PAUL WALL**

I work hard every day, earning income by doing whatever I have to do to get by. As a result of my effort, I am able to pile up the money I make as if it were slices of food made by mixing water with ground flour.

MORE CHEESE THAN LAMBEAU

LYRIC FROM SONG: **"CHECK 1, 2"** ON ALBUM: **OUT OF BUSINESS** BY ARTIST: **EPMD**

The amount of money I have is much greater than the number of hats shaped like a type of milk-derived, protein-rich food worn by fans in support of the Green Bay Packers football team in their stadium in Wisconsin, a state known for its dairy products.

NEEDED MONEY OF MY OWN, SO I STARTED SLANGIN'

LYRIC FROM SONG: **"DEAR MAMA"** ON ALBUM: **ME AGAINST THE WORLD** BY ARTIST: **2PAC**

For some people, there comes a time during their youth when they realize they can no longer live the lifestyle they want based solely on the support of individuals such as their mother who may provide for them, so they begin selling drugs as a way to survive and secure their own financial well-being.

BAG FULL OF CHIPS— WE AIN'T TALKIN' RUFFLES

LYRIC FROM SONG: **"THROW IT IN THE BAG"** ON ALBUM: **LOSO'S WAY** BY ARTIST: **FABOLOUS**

I have a bag that contains a large amount of paper money that I am describing by using a term that stems from the circular disks casinos use as in-house currency, clarifying that it is not a particular brand of thin crinkle-cut potato slices that you may have thought I was referring to.

THAT PABLO ESCOBAR CRACK MONEY

LYRIC FROM SONG: **"MONEY"** ON ALBUM: **LAX** BY ARTIST: **THE GAME**

I am striving to accumulate the same amount of wealth an infamous Colombian drug lord had at the height of his career—somewhere in the billions of dollars.

YOU CAN CALL ME SCROOGE, 'CAUSE I'M SWIMMIN' IN BUCKS

LYRIC FROM SONG: **"TALKIN' ABOUT IT"** ON ALBUM: **THE LEAK** BY ARTIST: **LIL WAYNE**

Since I have a great deal of money, you may wish to refer to me by the first name of a talking duck from comics and cartoons who has a vault room filled with gold coins, jewels, and cash, which he swan-dives into and tunnels through like he's swimming, since I might be able to do the same.

I GOT A POCKETFUL OF BENJAMINS

LYRIC FROM SONG: **"AIN'T SAYIN' NOTHIN' (REMIX)"**   BY ARTIST: **FAT JOE**

A compartment sewn into my clothing is full of hundred-dollar bills, which is the largest denomination currently in circulation and upon which are printed the face of Benjamin Franklin.

Y'ALL THINK I'M GONNA LET MY DOUGH FREEZE?

LYRIC FROM SONG: **"FORGOT ABOUT DRE"**   ON ALBUM: **2001**   BY ARTIST: **DR. DRE**

I am not asking your opinion on whether or not I should preserve a mixture of flour and water at cold temperatures for future use, but I would like to know if you think my savings balance will stay fixed at its current amount or if such an assumption could be false, considering that I am obviously going to continue making a lot of money.

MY BANK ROLL'S ON SWOLL

LYRIC FROM SONG: **"WHO AM I (WHAT'S MY NAME)?"**   ON ALBUM: **DOGGYSTYLE**
BY ARTIST: **SNOOP DOGGY DOGG**

The pile of bills I have rolled up and placed in my pocket and to which I add newly acquired currency, that I later withdraw money from like someone might use a lending institution, has increased in size as a result of my repeated business dealings.

I'M HOOD RICH

LYRIC FROM SONG: "STILL FLY"   ON ALBUM: HOOD RICH   BY ARTIST: **BIG TYMERS**

Although not considered especially wealthy when compared
to the likes of those in the upper echelon of society, I do well in
comparison to the others in my neighborhood. Some signs of my
wealth may include having a very expensive car yet not being able
to afford to fill the tank with gas, or making all large purchases by
obtaining loans using my mother as a cosigner.

GOT A HANDFUL OF STACKS, BETTER GRAB AN UMBRELLA

LYRIC FROM SONG: **"MAKE IT RAIN"** ON ALBUM: **ME, MYSELF & I** BY ARTIST: **FAT JOE**

When someone has a handful of paper money that is taken from piles that are considered disposable income and throws it above your head to create an effect that somewhat resembles rain falling from the sky, and you are an attractive female or an adoring fan, you may want to protect yourself by holding a canopy attached to a rod.

FROM A CAPER GOTTA BLOW THAT PAPER

LYRIC FROM SONG: **"CARTER II"**   ON ALBUM: **THA CARTER II**   BY ARTIST: **LIL WAYNE**

If money in your possession has made its way to your pocket either directly from a crime you committed or indirectly through your association with someone who may have committed a crime to obtain it, you should spend it as quickly as possible in case it can be traced and implicate you.

DRUGS
AND
ALCOHOL

SAW ME COOKIN' EGGS, SHE THOUGHT I WAS BACK AT IT

LYRIC FROM SONG: "STUNTIN' LIKE MY DADDY"   ON ALBUM: LIKE FATHER, LIKE SON
BY ARTIST: **BIRDMAN AND LIL WAYNE**

After spending the night with a woman, waking up in the morning, and making my way to the kitchen to prepare breakfast, I was seen standing in front of the stove by my female guest. Rather than investigating the situation to see that I was merely being a good host and cooking a meal for her and myself, she jumped to the conclusion that I was using the skillet in the manufacture of crack cocaine.

COUPLE BRICKS STACKED ON THAT TRIPLE BEAM

LYRIC FROM SONG: **"MAKE IT RAIN"** ON ALBUM: **ME, MYSELF & I** BY ARTIST: **FAT JOE**

I casually observe that among my surroundings are two large, rectangular solids of cocaine placed on the same type of very accurate scale used by scientists to measure the masses of things, either to make sure that enough product has been received in exchange for money spent, or that excess product is not provided when dividing up large quantities of a drug into smaller amounts for sale or distribution.

STANDIN' IN MY BATHROOM MIRROR, I LOOK AT THE SOAP

LYRIC FROM SONG: **"DUMMY MAN"**   ON ALBUM: **THUG MENTALITY 1999**
BY ARTIST: **KRAYZIE BONE**

During a moment of self-reflection while readying myself for the day, an idea strikes me: Because I am willing to risk my reputation and possibly even my life in order to obtain the funds required to purchase some marijuana, I might be able to cut a bar-shaped cleaning agent into tiny pieces, rub them with a slice of bread, and coat them in a numbing agent to make them resemble rocks of crack cocaine that I can sell to an unsuspecting individual.

BE FLIPPIN' THEM FLOUNDERS

LYRIC FROM SONG: **"REPPIN MY CITY"** ON ALBUM: **TRILLA** BY ARTIST: **RICK ROSS**

A concept I may or may not be familiar with is the act of receiving, processing into solid form or dividing into smaller quantities, and selling (resulting in orders that are placed for this product being filled) a high-quality type of cocaine named because in its shiny appearance it may seem to some to resemble the scales of a species of fish commonly found in the ocean.

BURNIN' BUTTER GOT IT SMELLIN' LIKE IT'S BUTTERSCOTCH

LYRIC FROM SONG: **"RICH OFF COCAINE"** ON ALBUM: **DEEPER THAN RAP** BY ARTIST: **RICK ROSS**

Someone has ignited a type of crack cocaine, presumably to inhale it, that has been refined to be more potent and is somewhat yellowish in color. The resulting scent is reminiscent of the brown-sugar-and-butter flavoring used in a variety of foods, including sundae toppings, pudding snacks, and a somewhat antiquated candy.

THAT BIRD FLU, SHAWTY, THAT'S A TERRIBLE SICKNESS

LYRIC FROM SONG: **"BIRD FLU"** ON ALBUM: **BACK TO THE TRAPHOUSE**
BY ARTIST: **GUCCI MANE**

While avian influenza is indeed a serious disease, when individuals begin selling cocaine and realize sudden and substantial financial gains are being made, it is difficult to stop what they are doing and pursue other work through traditional channels of employment.

I GOT FIVE ON IT, GRAB YOUR FOUR-OH, LET'S GET KEYED

LYRIC FROM SONG: **"I GOT 5 ON IT"** ON ALBUM: **OPERATION STACKOLA** BY ARTIST: **LUNIZ**

I have five dollars that I will contribute toward the purchase of an amount of marijuana we can smoke, and since I'm sure you have purchased affordable malt liquor in a bottle more than a liter in size to accompany the marijuana, please retrieve it and meet me back here so we can get high and intoxicated together.

A SCALE AND SOME ARM & HAMMER

LYRIC FROM SONG: "B.O.B." ON ALBUM: STANKONIA BY ARTIST: OUTKAST

One item that is handy to have around when producing crack cocaine from powder cocaine is a device to weigh quantities of ingredients used in this manufacturing process and to measure the final product, which is often sold by weight rather than volume. Another useful item is a particular brand of sodium bicarbonate that you may keep in your refrigerator to absorb and eliminate food odors but can also be used as part of the chemical reaction that transforms said drug substance from powder to crystalline form.

WHAT YOU KNOW ABOUT PURPLE DRANK?

LYRIC FROM SONG: **"THEY DON'T KNOW"**   ON ALBUM: **THE PEOPLES CHAMP**
BY ARTIST: **PAUL WALL**

I wonder if you are at all familiar with a practice that was popularized in the southern United States and is common in other parts of the country whereby a person mixes prescription cough syrup containing promethazine and codeine that may be purple in color with lemon-lime soda, fruit-flavored candies, or other flavorings to make its taste more palatable.

NO SEEDS, NO STEMS, NO STICKS

LYRIC FROM SONG: **"STILL D.R.E."** ON ALBUM: **2001** BY ARTIST: **DR. DRE**

Someone has made sure that the marijuana that has been obtained
is the best value for the money, containing no undesirable parts
of the cannabis plant and, being free of impurities, when smoked
allows one to experience the most pleasurable effects.

CHUMPS ACTIN' NIMBLE 'CAUSE THEY'RE FULL OF EIGHT-BALL

LYRIC FROM SONG: **"ICE ICE BABY"**   ON ALBUM: **TO THE EXTREME**   BY ARTIST: **VANILLA ICE**

Foolish individuals who may normally move and think sluggishly because of their slow reflexes or low level of intelligence are acting excitedly because they have ingested some portion of the eighth of an ounce of cocaine they have purchased.

SMOKIN' INDO, SIPPIN' ON GIN AND JUICE

LYRIC FROM SONG: **"GIN AND JUICE"**   ON ALBUM: **DOGGYSTYLE**
BY ARTIST: **SNOOP DOGGY DOGG**

High-quality cannabis imported from the country of Indonesia has been chosen to light and inhale. While there are other varieties of marijuana that may compare to this, the aforementioned strain complements my beverage of choice for this evening: alcohol mixed with orange juice, either in a ratio that I have chosen or that has been purchased premixed in a proportion that is to my liking.

COME TO VIP AND GET A CHAMPAGNE SHOWER

LYRIC FROM SONG: **"MONEY TO BLOW"**   ON ALBUM: **PRICELE$$**   BY ARTIST: **BIRDMAN**

Making your way to the part of the club or bar reserved for very important persons will not be in vain, because upon arrival you will be sprayed with carbonated wine, following which you might be permitted to dance with and talk to people you admire, or consume alcohol rather than having it poured on you.

I'M JUST HUSTLING IN THE STREETS TRYIN' TO FLIP A COUPLE KEES

LYRIC FROM SONG: **"SLOW DOWN"** ON ALBUM: **CARNIVAL VOL. II: MEMOIRS OF AN IMMIGRANT** BY ARTIST: **WYCLEF JEAN**

One school of thought concerning the concept of working energetically and quickly to take two kilograms or so of cocaine that has been purchased, possibly cooking it to make it into crack cocaine, and pricing the representative salable-sized chunks of this supply into cash, thereby making a profit in the process, is that such behavior should not be looked down upon.

I WANT Y'ALL BUCK NAKED WHILE Y'ALL COOKIN' UP MY DOPE

LYRIC FROM SONG: "GHETTO D" ON ALBUM: GHETTO D BY ARTIST: **MASTER P**

It is best that you remove all your clothing while in the kitchen, so you aren't tempted to take the crack cocaine you are making for yourself, and so that no one will wrongfully accuse you of doing so, since you will have no pockets. Also, if you are a female with an attractive body, you will be nice to look at.

RUBIK'S CUBE, YOU KNOW WE KEEP THEM WHITE SQUARES

LYRIC FROM SONG: **"STILL ON IT"**   ON ALBUM: **THE INSPIRATION**   BY ARTIST: **YOUNG JEEZY**

A six-sided puzzle toy invented in the 1970s is solved when each side shows nine of the same color of square-shaped stickers: red, orange, yellow, green, blue, and also white, which happens to be the color of a type of drug that is often distributed in packages with six sides.

151 AND COKE IS VIAGRA

LYRIC FROM SONG: **"IMMA TELL"**   ON ALBUM: **ABSOLUTE POWER**   BY ARTIST: **TECH N9NE**

Because its consumption in the vicinity of females often results in my arousal, a high-proof rum containing approximately 75 percent alcohol by volume combined with a certain type of cola-flavored soda pop seems to have the same effect on my anatomy as a drug used to combat erectile dysfunction.

WHAT YOU KNOW 'BOUT PUTTIN' BRICKS IN THE SPARE, MAN?

LYRIC FROM SONG: **"STUNTIN' LIKE MY DADDY"**   ON ALBUM: **LIKE FATHER, LIKE SON**
BY ARTIST: **BIRDMAN AND LIL WAYNE**

I ask you a rhetorical question about the idea of opening the trunk of your car and placing large amounts of cocaine in packages inside, under, and around the extra tire stored there and in other inconspicuous places for transportation, because I know you most likely don't have any knowledge about such a thing—although if you do, maybe we could discuss it.

IN THE KITCHEN COOKIN' CHICKEN

LYRIC FROM SONG: **"I MOVE CHICKENS"** ON ALBUM: **BACK TO THE TRAPHOUSE** BY ARTIST: **GUCCI MANE**

One could be in a particular room of the house to prepare omnivorous fowl for a meal, or one could be processing cocaine by following a recipe that turns it from powdered form into crack rocks.

THE RE-UPS BE LIKE BIRTHDAY PARTIES

LYRIC FROM SONG: **"FEEL ME"** ON ALBUM: **THA CARTER II** BY ARTIST: **LIL WAYNE**

When new shipments of drugs arrive in the neighborhood to be distributed to sales associates and subsequently sold to residents and visitors to the area, the reception among members of the community is one of great joy and celebration reminiscent of the celebration friends and families hold for a person who lives for another year.

INSULTS

DRINK KOOL-AID WITH THE ICE ON YOUR ARM

LYRIC FROM SONG: **"CALI SUNSHINE"**   ON ALBUM: **LAX**   BY ARTIST: **THE GAME**

The diamonds from the bracelet you have on your wrist might be something you feel proud to show off, but if they had the same liquid-cooling abilities of the ice cubes they resemble, my friends and I would drop them in a beverage marketed primarily to children.

CALL ME PAC-MAN, YOUR GHOSTS IS BLUE

LYRIC FROM SONG: **"FLY IN"** ON ALBUM: **THA CARTER II** BY ARTIST: **LIL WAYNE**

If we compared our situation to a video game, I would be a yellow pie-shaped character who glides around a maze eating dots, and you would be a red or pastel-colored ghost named Inky, Pinky, Blinky, or Clyde, who, because I have recently eaten a large power pellet, is now the same color as the clothing worn by a gang I am not affiliated with and running away from me because you are scared.

I WAS STRAPPED WIT' GATS WHEN YOU WERE CUDDLIN' A CABBAGE PATCH

LYRIC FROM SONG: **"FORGOT ABOUT DRE"** ON ALBUM: **2001** BY ARTIST: **DR. DRE**

When you were still a child and had no concerns other than playing with dolls in the comfort and safety of your home, I was carrying guns around to defend myself in my dangerous urban neighborhood.

GOT THE DOUGH YOU GET A YEAR STASHED IN MY SOCK DRAWER

LYRIC FROM SONG: **"MY LIFE YOUR ENTERTAINMENT"** ON ALBUM: **PAPER TRAIL** BY ARTIST: **T.I.**

The amount of money you earn after working for fifty-two weeks is equal to the small amount I have set aside for an emergency situation in one of the compartments in a piece of furniture where I store my underclothes.

THINKIN' SHE NUMBER ONE, WHEN SHE WAS JUST A JUMP-OFF

LYRIC FROM SONG: **"DRIVIN' ME WILD"**   ON ALBUM: **FINDING FOREVER**   BY ARTIST: **COMMON**

A woman thought she was the most important individual in a man's life because of his words, his actions, or a romantic encounter, but in fact she was only a temporary infatuation of his and, after engaging in sexual relations with her, he leaped out of bed with no intention of contacting her again.

YOU GON' BE THAT NEXT CHUMP TO END UP IN THE TRUNK

LYRIC FROM SONG: **"IF I CAN'T"**   ON ALBUM: **GET RICH OR DIE TRYIN'**   BY ARTIST: **50 CENT**

If you don't put a stop to actions or statements that are seen as aggressive or foolish, someone could decide to place you in the rearmost compartment of a car and transport you to a remote destination unbeknownst to you to be let out in whatever condition, should that be living or dead.

ELEVATOR TO THE TOP— SEE YA LATER

LYRIC FROM SONG: **"STILL NOT A PLAYER"**   ON ALBUM: **CAPITAL PUNISHMENT**
BY ARTIST: **BIG PUN**

I bid farewell to you for now from the lobby of a hotel, because it is getting late and I may have a woman to entertain or other activities to take care of before I retire for the night. I will be traveling all the way to the top floor of this building and arrive at my luxurious penthouse suite, while you either go home or to a standard hotel room on a lower floor. I leave with a courteous salutation that may or may not be genuine or come true should I pass within proximity of you in the future.

YOUR HOMIES WILL HAFTA POUR OUT A LITTLE LIQUOR

LYRIC FROM SONG: "CAN'T DENY IT"   ON ALBUM: GHETTO FABOLOUS   BY ARTIST: **FABOLOUS**

Because you are unable to defend yourself, friends of yours will be engaging in a ritualistic urban practice in which an amount of alcohol, usually malt liquor, is poured from its bottle onto the ground in your remembrance—a tribute to your life, which is now over.

CAB FARE? NO, HOPE YOUR TRAIN PASS WORKIN'

LYRIC FROM SONG: "ALL THE CHICKENS"   ON ALBUM: S.D.E.   BY ARTIST: **CAM'RON**

Female, I will not be driving you to your destination, nor will I be providing you with money to take a taxi, so for your sake it would be nice if you had a valid form of admittance for the subway or some other means of public transportation to get home.

YOU LIVE IN A DOLLHOUSE

LYRIC FROM SONG: **"I'M SO PAID"**   ON ALBUM: **FREEDOM**   BY ARTIST: **AKON**

Your home is miniature by comparison to mine and by my standards is not even suitable to be inhabited by human beings. Because your house also contains furniture and other items that I see as mere toys, I say this to emphasize that I am wealthier than you.

SHE GOT ONE OF YOUR KIDS, GOT YOU FOR EIGHTEEN YEARS

LYRIC FROM SONG: **"GOLD DIGGER"**   ON ALBUM: **LATE REGISTRATION**
BY ARTIST: **KANYE WEST**

Since you have gone against my advice and impregnated a woman, you will be receiving a constant reminder of your bad decision by having to pay child support to the mother of your child, whom you probably do not love, until the child is legally an adult.

WOULDN'T BUST A GRAPE IN A FRUIT FIGHT

LYRIC FROM SONG: **"99 PROBLEMS"**   ON ALBUM: **THE BLACK ALBUM**   BY ARTIST: **JAY-Z**

When I get into fights, things like guns and fists are involved. So I'm not afraid of you, because even if a fight ensued in which people were using food as weapons, you would be too scared to break a small piece of fruit or pull it out of your pocket unexpectedly, and possibly both.

YOUR RHYMES ARE FAKE LIKE A CANAL STREET WATCH

LYRIC FROM SONG: **"HEY FUCK YOU"**   ON ALBUM: **TO THE 5 BOROUGHS**
BY ARTIST: **BEASTIE BOYS**

The lyrics you vocalize in your songs are not truly representative of your behavior and therefore remind me of the imposter timepieces sold on a certain thoroughfare in the Manhattan borough of New York City.

GETTIN' WHAT YOU GET FOR A BRICK TO TALK GREASY

LYRIC FROM SONG: **"WANKSTA"** ON ALBUM: **GET RICH OR DIE TRYIN'** BY ARTIST: **50 CENT**

I easily make a lot of money rapping, as lyrics quickly come to mind and flow out of my mouth smoothly, and the amount of time it has taken me to earn this quantity is much shorter than the long hours you work selling the constituent parts of a large package of cocaine in many small transactions, which is difficult work for you.

RECORD LABELS SLANG OUR TAPES LIKE DOPE

LYRIC FROM SONG: **"IT'S BIGGER THAN HIP-HOP (REMIX)"** ON ALBUM: **LET'S GET FREE** BY ARTIST: **DEAD PREZ**

The companies that market our albums to consumers treat our artistic endeavors as if they were highly addictive drugs, not caring about the quality of the product but only focused on profits and convincing the masses to accept (and rappers to conform to) a certain style of music and lyrics that avoid discussing certain important topics.

THEY DON'T NEVER REALLY WANNA POP THEM THANGS

LYRIC FROM SONG: **"SATURDAY (OOOH OOOOH!)"** ON ALBUM: **WORD OF MOUF** BY ARTIST: **LUDACRIS**

Certain persons possess or wield guns in an attempt to intimidate others or to appear brave, while in fact they never intend on using their weapons, which, if discharged, would create a sudden loud noise that could cause them to regret what they've done and possibly soil their underpants.

G'S UP
HOES DOWN

LYRIC FROM SONG: "GIN AND JUICE"   ON ALBUM: DOGGYSTYLE
BY ARTIST: **SNOOP DOGGY DOGG**

It is good practice to elevate fellow gangsters who are few in
number to a position of equality and respect and to place no value
on women of questionable reputation who are many in number.
Regarding males and females who don't fall into either of these
categories, I don't have any recommendations.

BEEN SERVIN' SINCE YOU WAS DOIN' THE RUNNIN' MAN

LYRIC FROM SONG: **"RUBBER BAND MAN"**   ON ALBUM: **TRAP MUZIK**   BY ARTIST: **T.I.**

My experience selling drugs began long ago, at which point I quickly grew mature well beyond my years, while you were still concerning yourself with immature behavior like performing silly dances during which you looked like you were running in place.

YOUR BABY MAMA STILL GIVIN' ME BRAIN

LYRIC FROM SONG: **"THE WAY WE BALL"**   ON ALBUM: **UNDAGROUND LEGEND**
BY ARTIST: **LIL' FLIP**

The woman who is your child's mother continues to perform sexual favors for me on a somewhat regular basis, even though I am aware that you may be in a relationship with her. Even if you aren't still seeing her, you most likely have a lifelong emotional connection, and for me to tell you about our sexual indiscretions is very disrespectful.

LEAVE YOU KINDA STARTLED LIKE THE FUNK OFF OF FRITOS

LYRIC FROM SONG: **"DITTY"**   ON ALBUM: **THE NINE YARDS**   BY ARTIST: **PAPERBOY**

Because you are relatively inexperienced, my actions will surprise you as if you had inhaled the pungent aroma from a just-opened bag of a particular brand of strong-smelling corn chips.

CARS

INSIDE FISH STICKS, OUTSIDE TARTAR SAUCE

LYRIC FROM SONG: **"PUT ON"** ON ALBUM: **THE RECESSION** BY ARTIST: **YOUNG JEEZY**

My car's interior upholstery is a very unique tan or beige color that I can help you visualize by comparing it to the color of a piece of breaded and deep-fried seafood. The complementary paint on the exterior is a shade of white that is very glossy and can be best described as the color of a condiment you most likely dip the afore-mentioned food in.

LEATHER GUTS AND THE FISHBOWL

LYRIC FROM SONG: **"WHAT YOU KNOW"** ON ALBUM: **KING** BY ARTIST: **T.I.**

While some people like to have their vehicle's windows tinted for the purpose of heat reduction, reduced outside-in visibility, or other considerations, I like the windows of my car to remain transparent so that people can observe and admire me and the upholstery lin-ing much of the interior of my car, which is made from animal skin because I consider cloth and vinyl to be inferior fabrics.

RIMS KEEP SPINNIN' EVERY TIME I STOP

LYRIC FROM SONG: **"STILL FLY"**   ON ALBUM: **HOOD RICH**   BY ARTIST: **BIG TYMERS**

I have installed special aftermarket wheels on my car, parts of which continue to rotate even after the car comes to a complete stop—a result of forward momentum that has built up while driving coupled with the reduced friction of the ball-bearing system they use. This is intriguing to people and draws attention to me and my vehicle because it is not commonly seen and creates an illusion of forward travel while the car is stationary.

TRYIN' TO CATCH ME RIDIN' DIRTY

LYRIC FROM SONG: **"RIDIN'"**   ON ALBUM: **THE SOUND OF REVENGE**
BY ARTIST: **CHAMILLIONAIRE**

Law enforcement officers are unfairly targeting me because of jealousy or racial profiling, watching for a relatively unimportant traffic violation or vehicular infraction in order to have a legally justifiable reason to pull me over and attempt to search my person or car, which may or may not contain controlled substances, unregistered firearms, or other illegal items.

HAVE THE PARKIN' LOT ON SMASH

LYRIC FROM SONG: **"THE BOSS"**   ON ALBUM: **TRILLA**   BY ARTIST: **RICK ROSS**

The surface of the parking lot could be said to be under great pressure from the amount of people congregating there, and the noise level has increased as people have started to gather. There is plenty of space for many automobiles and for people to mingle to talk about current events, socialize, and show off. Because this place is not associated with any particular person's residence, it is free of the liability associated with hosting a party or gathering at one's home, and because it may be somewhat centrally located, it can be a convenient place to rendezvous.

I USED TO HAVE TO GET MY STROLL ON

LYRIC FROM SONG: **"LET ME RIDE"**   ON ALBUM: **THE CHRONIC**   BY ARTIST: **DR. DRE**

Some time ago, before I was able to afford a nice vehicle to drive around in (and short of asking for rides from friends, taking the bus, or traveling in a taxicab to various places), I had to resort to the only viable form of transportation available: using my own two feet to casually walk from place to place.

FORD TAURUS PULL UP, EVERYBODY RUN

LYRIC FROM SONG: **"MY HOOD"**   ON ALBUM: **LET'S GET IT: THUG MOTIVATION 101**
BY ARTIST: **YOUNG JEEZY**

When a certain model of domestic sedan not known to be owned by someone in the neighborhood comes to a sudden halt near us, I suggest you flee, because it is a vehicle commonly driven by plain-clothes police officers, who are people we want to avoid.

IF I HIT THE SWITCH, I CAN MAKE THE ASS DROP

LYRIC FROM SONG: **"IT WAS A GOOD DAY"** ON ALBUM: **THE PREDATOR** BY ARTIST: **ICE CUBE**

If, from the driver's seat of my car or from outside the vehicle using a remote button, I trigger a certain combination of hydraulic pumps connected to my car's suspension, the result is that the rear end of the car will lower near to or even all the way to the ground, which is an amusing effect that almost certainly draws attention to me as I drive, sit in, or stand next to my car and may cause an interesting display of sparks as the metallic vehicle components contact the hard surface of the roadway or parking lot.

IF YOU IN THE WHIP, GHOST RIDE THE BITCH

LYRIC FROM SONG: **"KEEP BOUNCIN' (STREET)"**   ON ALBUM: **BLOW THE WHISTLE**
BY ARTIST: **TOO $HORT**

If you happen to be driving in your vehicle, it would be possible, while it continues to coast forward, to open the door, get out, and dance alongside the car or on top of the hood to show off to onlookers and effectively make it appear that the still-living soul of a deceased human being is controlling the car.

WHAT YOU THINK I RAP FOR, TO PUSH A FUCKIN' RAV4?

LYRIC FROM SONG: **"RUN THIS TOWN"**   ON ALBUM: **THE BLUEPRINT 3**   BY ARTIST: **JAY-Z**

Do you honestly think the motivation behind my music career is to be able to ultimately live a lifestyle in which my primary automobile is the Toyota RAV4 sport-utility vehicle? Toyotas may be dependable and stylish cars, but I think I deserve to reward myself with a different class of vehicle and have therefore set my sights on something more luxurious, such as Toyota's high-end Lexus line.

IN MY SLAB PUFFIN' POUNDS, TRYIN' TA TAKE AWAY MY FROWN

LYRIC FROM SONG: **"TOP DROP"**   ON ALBUM: **BOSS OF ALL BOSSES**   BY ARTIST: **SLIM THUG**

I am in my car, a place in which I frequently seek refuge when life has me feeling down, smoking very large amounts of marijuana, reflecting upon recent events, and trying to forget about my troubles in order to see things in a more positive light.

TRUNK BUMP LIKE CHICKEN POX

LYRIC FROM SONG: **"SITTIN' SIDEWAYZ"**   ON ALBUM: **THE PEOPLES CHAMP**
BY ARTIST: **PAUL WALL**

I use onomatopoeia to liken the repetitive, thumping, low-frequency tones the speakers in the rear compartment of my vehicle are making as they reproduce a musical recording to the raised sores resulting from a contagious infection of varicella zoster virus that is common during childhood.

WINDOWS SO DARK, YOU NEED A FLASHLIGHT TO SEE ME

LYRIC FROM SONG: "BOURBONS AND LACS"   ON ALBUM: GHÉTTO D   BY ARTIST: **MASTER P**

The thin, semitransparent film I have applied to my car's windows is not necessarily to prevent the car from getting hot during the summer, to prevent harmful ultraviolet rays from reaching the interior, or just to be stylish, but primarily so that no one can identify me when I am inside without the aid of a cylindrical, battery-powered illumination device.

SUMITOMO TIRES AND THEY GOTTA BE RUN FLAT

LYRIC FROM SONG: "STILL FLY"   ON ALBUM: HOOD RICH   BY ARTIST: **BIG TYMERS**

I require a specific brand of high-quality tires to be fitted on the aftermarket wheels I have installed on my vehicle, which are of a special type that even if punctured can still be driven on for a period of time, allowing me to maneuver my car out of harm's way or to a place that is safer than my current location.

WATCH THE CANDY PAINT CHANGE EVERY TIME I SWITCH LANES

LYRIC FROM SONG: **"RIDE WIT ME"** ON ALBUM: **COUNTRY GRAMMAR** BY ARTIST: **NELLY**

Keep your attention fixed on the exterior of my car from a relatively stationary position, such as the sidewalk or a more slowly moving vehicle, and you may notice that as I change the position of my car relative to you and the sun or another constant light source, the polychromatic, pearlescent paint that has been applied will change color before your eyes.

MY WEST COAST SHORTY PUSH THE CHROME 740

LYRIC FROM SONG: **"IT'S ALL ABOUT THE BENJAMINS (REMIX)"** ON ALBUM: **NO WAY OUT**
BY ARTIST: **PUFF DADDY & THE FAMILY**

The female I associate with while I am spending time in California is driving a high-end BMW brand automobile, which I may have purchased for or loaned to her, and that has had a special coating applied to give it an extremely bright, silver, mirrorlike finish.

MORE TVS IN HERE THAN WHERE I LIVE

LYRIC FROM SONG: **"DRIVE SLOW"** ON ALBUM: **LATE REGISTRATION**
BY ARTIST: **KANYE WEST**

Because of my active social life and the possibility that I spend a limited amount of time sitting around at home, I may only care to have a television in the living room, the bedroom, and a few other areas of my house that are practical. In my car, though, where video viewing may be more a matter of pride than convenience, I have screens densely located throughout its interior, on surfaces such as the dashboard, steering wheel, sun visors, headrests, ceiling, trunk, and possibly other places, but which I would probably not view while driving, as I would not want to violate any local laws.

SLIDE, SLIDE, SLIPPITY-SLIDE, WITH SWITCHES ON THE BLOCK IN A '65

LYRIC FROM SONG: **"FANTASTIC VOYAGE"**   ON ALBUM: **IT TAKES A THIEF**   BY ARTIST: **COOLIO**

I am driving a 1965 model car around on the streets of my neighborhood with a system of hydraulic pumps connected to its suspension that, when activated, make various corners of the car, one side of the car, the front or back of the car, or the entire body of the car raise or lower to show off to pedestrians or other drivers as I glide smoothly down the road.

KNOCKIN' DOWN PICTURES OFF YA WALL

LYRIC FROM SONG: **"BEAT'N DOWN YO BLOCK"**   ON ALBUM: **BEAT'N DOWN YO BLOCK!**
BY ARTIST: **UNK**

The bass coming from the low-frequency subwoofer speakers
in the trunk of my car is so loud that not only does it most likely
awaken you from your slumber, interrupt your conversation or television viewing, and rattle the windows of your house, but the sound
waves vibrate against your home so forcefully that any framed
photographs or artwork you have hung inside will fall down when I
drive past.

USED TO COUNT MY SPOKES, NOW THESE HOES COUNT MY INCHES

LYRIC FROM SONG: **"WANNA BE A BALLER"** ON ALBUM: **SITTIN' FAT DOWN SOUTH** BY ARTIST: **LIL' TROY**

Years ago, females I would not consider as life partners but possibly as temporary romantic acquaintances showed me respect by counting the dozens of thin metal pieces they saw radiating outward from the center of the smaller-diameter gold wheels that were on my car. Now that having larger-diameter solid chrome wheels is more popular, these same individuals show their admiration by taking note of the wheels' diameter using the English system of measurement.

SEX
AND
RELATIONSHIPS

I'M NOT A PLAYER, I JUST CRUSH A LOT

LYRIC FROM SONG: **"STILL NOT A PLAYER"**   ON ALBUM: **CAPITAL PUNISHMENT**
BY ARTIST: **BIG PUN**

Although I may engage in frequent sexual encounters with women for pleasure, this does not mean I fall into the category of those who use clever language to get females into bed. I may or may not attribute this behavior to my habit of easily becoming emotionally invested in females I have recently met.

I LOVE YOU LIKE A FAT KID LOVE CAKE

LYRIC FROM SONG: **"21 QUESTIONS"**   ON ALBUM: **GET RICH OR DIE TRYIN'**   BY ARTIST: **50 CENT**

The passionate affection I feel toward you is as great as the pleasure an obese child finds in eating a delicious pastry.

HOLLA AT A HOE 'TIL I GOT A BITCH CONFUSED

LYRIC FROM SONG: "P.I.M.P."   ON ALBUM: **GET RICH OR DIE TRYIN'**   BY ARTIST: **50 CENT**

I will speak with a commanding presence and be assertive to get a female's attention, using a line of questioning and compliments that result in her becoming so puzzled that she accepts my suggestions to prevent embarrassment or because she thought she was agreeing to something else.

WAY YOU DROP, WOULDA THOUGHT I HAD A TASER

LYRIC FROM SONG: **"DEY KNOW"**   ON ALBUM: **UNITS IN THE CITY**   BY ARTIST: **SHAWTY LO**

The manner in which you are quickly lowering your posterior toward the floor and the flexibility you display for me in the process might cause onlookers to form the mistaken impression that your body was moving that way involuntarily as a result of the electrical current flowing through it delivered from a weapon used to neutralize criminals.

EVEN THUGS GET LONELY

LYRIC FROM SONG: **"TEMPTATIONS"**   ON ALBUM: **ME AGAINST THE WORLD**   BY ARTIST: **2PAC**

Although it might not cross your mind due to some of the things I say and because I act tough and convey an image that might seem emotionless, there are times when I long for the company of a loving woman or a friend to share my troubles and innermost feelings with.

I'LL BAG YOU LIKE SOME GROCERIES

LYRIC FROM SONG: **"LOVE IN THIS CLUB"**   ON ALBUM: **HERE I STAND**   BY ARTIST: **USHER**

I will get you into the metaphorical sack, containing you within the covers of my bed, as easily as I would place a recently purchased item from the local supermarket into a paper, plastic, or reusable canvas shopping bag.

MY TIME IS HELD UP EXTREMELY FOR COOKIES

LYRIC FROM SONG: **"DITTY"** ON ALBUM: **THE NINE YARDS** BY ARTIST: **PAPERBOY**

I am not necessarily bothered that the majority of my schedule is dedicated to or my progress is frequently impeded by attractive young women who either pursue me or whom I pursue.

THE JOCKS GET THE FLY GIRLS, AND ME, I GET THE HOOD RATS

LYRIC FROM SONG: **"I WISH"** ON ALBUM: **I WISH** BY ARTIST: **SKEE-LO**

Males who excel at sports such as basketball receive the privilege of being involved with attractive females, whereas, because I am not skilled in sports, I am left with females who are similar to rodents in that they are commonly found around the neighborhood and do not always pay close attention to personal hygiene.

BITCHES DON'T SAY NO TO ME, I'M LIKE A WEDDING RING

LYRIC FROM SONG: **"DOPE BOYS"** ON ALBUM: **LAX** BY ARTIST: **THE GAME**

Women do not ever disagree with anything I say nor the things I suggest, because I am as profound as a marriage proposal when I speak, resulting in their speechlessness or acceptance of my suggestions with an affirmative reply.

GIVE GOOD BRAIN LIKE YOU GRADUATED FROM A GOOD SCHOOL

LYRIC FROM SONG: **"YOU"** ON ALBUM: **STREET LOVE** BY ARTIST: **LLOYD**

Even though I am aware sexual ability has no direct correlation to formal education, you perform fellatio very well, as if you have received a degree in the subject or have studied it at a prestigious educational institution.

PACK A VEST FOR YOUR JIMMY IN THE CITY OF SEX

LYRIC FROM SONG: "CALIFORNIA LOVE (REMIX)"   ON ALBUM: ALL EYEZ ON ME   BY ARTIST: 2PAC

If you have not chosen to abstain from sexual intercourse until after marriage, you should wear a condom—the sexual equivalent to a bulletproof vest and something that is highly necessary in Los Angeles, which is a place that has many people with sexually transmitted diseases.

IF YOU AIN'T NO PUNK, HOLLER "WE WANT PRENUP"

LYRIC FROM SONG: **"GOLD DIGGER"**   ON ALBUM: **LATE REGISTRATION**   BY ARTIST: **KANYE WEST**

If you are aware that a lot of women in this world are after men who are wealthy, insist upon signing a legal contract before marriage so that if the partnership ends in divorce, you will not lose any of your hard-earned money, which you acquired before meeting this female.

I WANNA HIT THAT MORE THAN I WANNA HIT THE LOTTO

LYRIC FROM SONG: **"ROCKIN' THAT SHIT (REMIX)"** ON ALBUM: **LOVE VS. MONEY** BY ARTIST: **THE-DREAM**

My desire to engage in intercourse with a particular woman is greater than my desire to be awarded millions of dollars as the result of numbers I have chosen being drawn in a game of chance.

YOU DON'T STRIKE ME AS A WOMAN THAT FRONTS

LYRIC FROM SONG: **"AIN'T GONNA HURT NOBODY"** ON ALBUM: **FACE THE NATION** BY ARTIST: **KID 'N PLAY**

You do not seem as if you would put up verbal, emotional, or physical barriers to my approach, especially without previous knowledge of what my intentions are.

WITNESS ME HOLLER AT A HOOCHIE, SEE HOW QUICK THE GAME TAKES

LYRIC FROM SONG: **"ALL 'BOUT U"**   ON ALBUM: **ALL EYEZ ON ME**   BY ARTIST: **2PAC**

Sit back and observe as I engage in conversation with a woman of questionable sexual reputation and take note of how, by following conversational strategies that I have planned and adapted to my situation and my environment, only a short amount of time will elapse from the time I begin this activity until I convince her to do what I want.

SHORTY SENT A TWIT PIC SAYING COME AND GET THIS

LYRIC FROM SONG: **"LOL :-)"**   ON ALBUM: **READY**   BY ARTIST: **TREY SONGZ**

My female acquaintance, who is not as tall as I am, has used her mobile phone to transmit a seductive photograph to an Internet photo-sharing service that accompanies a popular microblogging Web site along with a text caption requesting I visit her for a romantic encounter.

HOOKERS LOOKIN' SO HARD, THEY STRAIGHT HIT THE CURB

LYRIC FROM SONG: **"REGULATE"**   ON ALBUM: **REGULATE . . . G FUNK ERA**   BY ARTIST: **WARREN G**

The driver of a vehicle whose passengers had their eyes fixed on my nice automobile was in such awe of me that she failed to maintain control of her vehicle and it came in contact with the raised portion of concrete separating the roadway from the sidewalk; resulting in her embarrassment.

IF I WASN'T MARRIED TO THE STREETS, IT'D BE YOU

LYRIC FROM SONG: **"BUST IT BABY, PART 2"**   ON ALBUM: **DEFINITION OF REAL**   BY ARTIST: **PLIES**

If my life didn't revolve around and wasn't dedicated to the urban matters of my neighborhood, you would be my second choice, but don't get your hopes up, because my priorities aren't likely to change anytime soon.

MY PHONY HOMIE HAD A BABY BY MY OWN GIRL BUT I AIN'T TRIPPIN', I'M A PLAYER

LYRIC FROM SONG: **"UNTIL THE END OF TIME"**   ON ALBUM: **UNTIL THE END OF TIME**
BY ARTIST: **2PAC**

I was under the impression that a person I knew was a good friend, but he turned out not to be as trustworthy as I originally thought, as I found out he impregnated my girlfriend. I didn't dwell on this, though, but instead moved on with my life because I have other females I can turn to for companionship.

TREAT YOU LIKE THE FIRST LADY— I'LL PUT MY BARACK IN YA

LYRIC FROM SONG: **"ROCKIN' THAT SHIT (REMIX)"**   ON ALBUM: **LOVE VS. MONEY**
BY ARTIST: **THE-DREAM**

I will take care of you as if you were married to the president of the United States, and the presidential treatment I give you will extend even to the bedroom, where I will pleasure you with my member which, because of the level of respect people show it, has been named after President Obama.

CRIME
AND
WEAPONS

HEARD THE BIRD CIRCLE WHILE I WAS EATING FISH AND WATCHING URKEL

LYRIC FROM SONG: **"GHETTO BIRD"**   ON ALBUM: **LETHAL INJECTION**   BY ARTIST: **ICE CUBE**

A police helicopter that was looking for me because I was a suspect in a crime was audible while I was hiding in a friend's house eating food acceptable according to the guidelines of the Islamic faith and focusing my attention on the television, specifically one of the characters from the 1990s sitcom *Family Matters.*

WE POP THEM TOASTERS

LYRIC FROM SONG: **"THE GAMBLER"**   ON ALBUM: **MAN VS MACHINE**   BY ARTIST: **XZIBIT**

We squeeze the triggers of guns as casually as if we were attempting to discharge bread from a kitchen appliance before it had reached the level of warmth and crispness associated with the setting we had selected.

I'M COMIN' WITH A GUN LIKE A NINTENDO

LYRIC FROM SONG: **"TALKIN' ABOUT IT"**   ON ALBUM: **THE LEAK**   BY ARTIST: **LIL WAYNE**

In the 1980s, a newly purchased Nintendo Entertainment System console commonly came with an electronic plastic light gun accessory that was used to play the bundled cartridge *Duck Hunt*, and although my weapon is not a toy, I take it many places.

BETTER TOSS THAT YAYO, KEEP YOUR BANKROLL

LYRIC FROM SONG: **"1ST OF THA MONTH"**   ON ALBUM: **E 1999 ETERNAL**
BY ARTIST: **BONE THUGS-N-HARMONY**

If you are being chased by the police, it is advisable to throw any cocaine you have on your person into the bushes or in some other hard-to-find location that you can return to later, because if caught you could be searched, and if an illegal substance is found in your possession, you could be charged with a crime. However, it is advisable that you hang on to the rolled-up stack of currency you have in your pocket, because it is not something that you can be charged with a crime for having.

GET SWISS-CHEESED UP

LYRIC FROM SONG: **"WHO SHOT YA"**   ON ALBUM: **GREATEST HITS**
BY ARTIST: **THE NOTORIOUS B.I.G.**

The amount of bullets that enter and exit you relative to your body's surface area will be great in number and in equal proportion to the number of holes in a slice of a particular type of milk-derived sandwich ingredient.

TRUNK OF THE CAR, WE GOT THE STREET-SWEEPER

LYRIC FROM SONG: **"MADE YOU LOOK"**   ON ALBUM: **GOD'S SON**   BY ARTIST: **NAS**

Our car is not large enough that a road-cleaning vehicle can fit in one of its compartments, but we may have an automatic weapon stored there capable of blanketing the entire street in gunfire.

GOT THE SCOOP ON HOW TO GET A BULLETPROOF

LYRIC FROM SONG: **"HOW DO U WANT IT"**   ON ALBUM: **ALL EYEZ ON ME**   BY ARTIST: **2PAC**

I am privy to information on how to obtain a vest that will protect you from gunshots, which not everyone knows how to obtain and could be essential in protecting you from enemy fire.

SEND A JACKER INTO A COMA

LYRIC FROM SONG: **"RIDIN'"** ON ALBUM: **THE SOUND OF REVENGE** BY ARTIST: **CHAMILLIONAIRE**

If a person approaches me with a weapon and is intent on taking control of my car and possibly harming me or my fellow passengers, they could be put into a state of indefinite unconsciousness through an act of self-defense.

GOT A PUMP UNDER MY SEAT, SAWED-OFF

LYRIC FROM SONG: **"I'M SO PAID"**   ON ALBUM: **FREEDOM**   BY ARTIST: **AKON**

A shotgun has been modified, its barrel shortened with a hacksaw in order to make it easier to conceal under the driver's seat of an automobile and also to widen the spread of its shot, which is handy for self-defense in close-range combat situations.

SOME BROTHERS PULLED SOME GATS, SO I SAID, "I'M STUCK"

LYRIC FROM SONG: **"REGULATE"**   ON ALBUM: **REGULATE . . . G FUNK ERA**   BY ARTIST: **WARREN G**

As I approached individuals I identified as likely to treat me like family, they brandished firearms and I realized I was in a difficult situation, which I was unable to remove myself from at that moment without assistance.

WHOLE CAR STRAPPED, AND I AIN'T TALKIN' SEAT BELTS

LYRIC FROM SONG: **"BOTTOM OF THE MAP"**   ON ALBUM: **LET'S GET IT: THUG MOTIVATION 101**
BY ARTIST: **YOUNG JEEZY**

Every individual sitting in the automobile has a gun, which, regardless of the adjective used, is probably not in a holster but more likely secured within the waistband of one's pants, and I am not making a reference to the safety devices protecting their lives in case of an accident.

SEVEN-TIME FELON, WHAT I CARE ABOUT A CASE, MAN?

LYRIC FROM SONG: **"RUBBER BAND MAN"** ON ALBUM: **TRAP MUZIK** BY ARTIST: **T.I.**

I have been charged with or convicted of over half a dozen serious crimes, so I am familiar with court proceedings and will remain calm if on trial or forced to serve time in a correctional facility.

GET A ID, THE NAME SAYS YOU BUT THE FACE IS ME

LYRIC FROM SONG: **"HELL YEAH"** ON ALBUM: **RBG: REVOLUTIONARY BUT GANGSTA**
BY ARTIST: **DEAD PREZ**

One way to exploit a corrupt system is to confuse law enforcement officers by falsifying driver's license information, making it difficult for investigators to pin a crime such as credit fraud on you.

GOT THE HOLLOW POINTS FOR THE SNITCHES

LYRIC FROM SONG: **"LET ME RIDE"**   ON ALBUM: **THE CHRONIC**   BY ARTIST: **DR. DRE**

Bullets with empty cavities on their tips that are particularly harmful are available to be used against people who decide to inform the police of possible suspects in crimes that have taken place.

I'M A FED, LIKE ALCOHOL, TOBACCO, AND FIREARMS

LYRIC FROM SONG: **"ROLLING WITH HEAT"** ON ALBUM: **PHRENOLOGY** BY ARTIST: **THE ROOTS**

I am interested in beverages, plants, and weapons, and while this shows that my interests are similar to those of a person employed by a certain government agency, I may be more concerned with the acquisition of these items than with enforcing the laws that govern their use.

TAP MY CELL AND THE PHONE IN THE BASEMENT

LYRIC FROM SONG: **"MO MONEY MO PROBLEMS"**   ON ALBUM: **LIFE AFTER DEATH**
BY ARTIST: **THE NOTORIOUS B.I.G.**

I am so successful in my various business ventures that I am a target of law enforcement surveillance in the form of the monitoring of my telephone calls, both my wireless handset and the second phone line installed in a part of my house where I might take care of business-related activities due to its distance from the front door and other home entry points.

YOU'LL KEEP YOUR MOUTH CLOSED, WE DON'T TOLERATE SNITCHES

LYRIC FROM SONG: **"NO SNITCHIN'"** ON ALBUM: **THE SOUND OF REVENGE** BY ARTIST: **CHAMILLIONAIRE**

Giving the police any information about a crime or identifying someone from your community as a suspect is considered an act of extreme disrespect regardless of what you may believe is a moral obligation, and may result in you being hated by the neighborhood.

PACK A FOUR-MATIC THAT CRACK YOUR WHOLE CABBAGE

LYRIC FROM SONG: **"LIFE'S A BITCH"** ON ALBUM: **ILLMATIC** BY ARTIST: **NAS**

Someone has stored a high-caliber automatic weapon that is entirely capable of damaging your head, which is roughly the size of a dense, leafy vegetable.

THAT PHOTO PHOBIA, NO KODAK MOMENTS

LYRIC FROM SONG: **"CARTER II"**   ON ALBUM: **THA CARTER II**   BY ARTIST: **LIL WAYNE**

While I don't have a particular fear of cameras themselves, I still do not want to be the subject or even in the background of any unnecessary photographs, even if a major film manufacturer suggested I should participate as part of an advertising campaign, because the more photos of me that are available, the more likely I can be identified and found after a crime that I may or may not have committed.

GUNS IN THE ATTIC, MAMA HELP ME PUT 'EM UP

LYRIC FROM SONG: **"RICH OFF COCAINE"** ON ALBUM: **DEEPER THAN RAP**
BY ARTIST: **RICK ROSS**

If I were to have a supply of firearms obtained by either legal or illegal means and wanted to store them somewhere I knew was safe, I would turn to my mother because she would help me hide them in the top floor of her house—that way they would be in a very unsuspicious location and if someone were to look for them, they would, presuming my mother protects me, have a difficult time finding them.

FASHION

SHOW MY FRONTS— IT'S MORE KARATS THAN BUGS BUNNY'S LUNCH

LYRIC FROM SONG: **"SITTIN' SIDEWAYZ"**   ON ALBUM: **THE PEOPLES CHAMP**
BY ARTIST: **PAUL WALL**

Direct your focus toward my anterior incisor and cuspid teeth, which are most visible when my mouth opens, and pay no attention to the molars and bicuspids, which may be easily visible. As you can see, the weight of the diamonds inset into my decorative mouthpiece is a larger number than the quantity of vegetables a cartoon rabbit would eat during his midday meal.

I HAD THE RED AND BLACK LUMBERJACK WITH THE HAT TO MATCH

LYRIC FROM SONG: **"JUICY"**   ON ALBUM: **READY TO DIE**   BY ARTIST: **THE NOTORIOUS B.I.G.**

My wardrobe previously consisted of a dual-colored wool coat and cap in a plaid pattern, which was a fashionable style popularized by men who cut down trees and, now that I have shifted my attention to more expensive things, is pleasing to me as I reminisce about my past and how my tastes have changed to match current fashion trends.

GOT MORE KARATS THAN AISLE D, MORE BREAD THAN AISLE G

LYRIC FROM SONG: "E.I."   ON ALBUM: **COUNTRY GRAMMAR**   BY ARTIST: **NELLY**

The weight and purity combined with the quantity of the expensive diamond or gold jewelry that is being worn is greater than the amount of vegetables and processed grains one would find in two arbitrarily chosen marked aisles at a grocery store.

I SPORT THE CHINCHILLA TO HURT THEY FEELINS

LYRIC FROM SONG: **"LEAN BACK"** ON ALBUM: **TRUE STORY** BY ARTIST: **TERROR SQUAD**

Although reasons to wear a coat made from the fur of a rodent are many, including enhancement of appearance, a feeling of comfort, and warmth against freezing temperatures, the main reason to wear this material is to show that you have a lot of money and can afford expensive things, thereby raising your self-esteem above that of others and making them feel sad and relatively insignificant.

SEE THE OYSTER PERPETUAL DAY-DATE

LYRIC FROM SONG: **"HI HATER"**   ON ALBUM: **IF TOMORROW COMES**   BY ARTIST: **MAINO**

Although most young people tend to use the clocks on their mobile phones to keep track of the time, you should take notice when someone wears a specific type of expensive high-quality Rolex wristwatch, whether for timekeeping or fashion, because they spent a lot of money on it and would feel more justified about the expense if you would compliment them or otherwise indicate that you have taken notice.

KEEP KNOCKIN', WHETHER YOU'RE LOU' VUITTON IT UP OR REEBOK-IN'

LYRIC FROM SONG: **"KNOCK YOU DOWN"**   ON ALBUM: **IN A PERFECT WORLD . . .**
BY ARTIST: **KERI HILSON**

Continue to put others down through your words or actions and without considering the brand of the clothing or shoes you are wearing, nor your associated socioeconomic status, thereby elevating yourself to a position of respect and success relative to them.

I'M DOWN TO DIE FOR MY CHAIN

LYRIC FROM SONG: **"IF I CAN'T"**   ON ALBUM: **GET RICH OR DIE TRYIN'**   BY ARTIST: **50 CENT**

Necklaces, although often worn as a fashion statement, do not always merely provide an enhancement to one's appearance—to some they are a representation of beliefs through association with a particular record label, lifestyle, or peer group in which one takes great pride, and defending oneself from the theft of such an item is something that will be done at all costs.

SO MUCH ICE ON THE WATCH, YOU WOULDA THOUGHT TIME FROZE

LYRIC FROM SONG: **"STILL ON IT"**   ON ALBUM: **THE INSPIRATION**   BY ARTIST: **YOUNG JEEZY**

Since both frozen water and highly compressed carbon share a similar luster, and since some people associate the lack of movement during a hypothetical pause in the space-time continuum to the cooling of water or another substance below thirty-two degrees Fahrenheit, you might think such an event is about to happen because of the large number of diamonds on the timepiece I wear on my wrist.

OPEN UP MY MOUTH AND SUNLIGHT ILLUMINATES THE DARK

LYRIC FROM SONG: "DRIVE SLOW"   ON ALBUM: LATE REGISTRATION   BY ARTIST: **KANYE WEST**

Should my lips part and expose what you would expect to be the enamel of my teeth, you will be surprised to find out that the diamond-covered mouthpiece I am wearing, while not a source of light itself, causes reflections from the sun or other light sources to illuminate dark areas around me. At the same time this is happening, you might also note that the words I am saying will cause you to be more aware of matters you may not have previously had information about.

SHE GOT THE GUCCI LINEN

LYRIC FROM SONG: **"HEY MA"** ON ALBUM: **COME HOME WITH ME** BY ARTIST: **CAM'RON**

A particular woman has procured designer-brand bed dressings, which is a delightful thing both because of her good taste in fashion and the close attention she pays to details such as the level of comfort guests feel when spending time in her bedroom and which I may appreciate when visiting for a romantic evening.

I'M A SUCKER FOR CORNROWS AND MANICURED TOES

LYRIC FROM SONG: **"E.I."** ON ALBUM: **COUNTRY GRAMMAR** BY ARTIST: **NELLY**

There is something about tightly braided strands of hair running from the forehead to the back of the neck and the expert grooming of the digits on the end of a woman's feet that show careful attention has been paid to her appearance and makes me excited to the point that my emotions overpower my mental reasoning and cause me to make some concessions regarding issues that I would normally stand my ground on.

LOUIS KNAPSACK WHERE I'M HOLDIN' ALL THE WORK AT

LYRIC FROM SONG: **"WHAT YOU KNOW"** ON ALBUM: **KING** BY ARTIST: **T.I.**

A female associate is carrying a Louis Vuitton brand designer bag, which is where a supply of drugs is temporarily stored, because it should not be kept on one's person until after confirmation that the client has the required funds to buy the drugs has taken place, at which point the woman can be cleared to approach the staging area with the product, the vicinity having been verified as safe so that the transaction can conclude.

WAY BACK, LIKE A SILK WIFE-BEATER AND A WAVE CAP

LYRIC FROM SONG: "LET THE BEAT BUILD"   ON ALBUM: THA CARTER III   BY ARTIST: LIL WAYNE

Some years ago it began being particularly stylish for individuals to wear undershirts made of exceptionally smooth material named after the type of males who engaged in spousal abuse and commonly wore them, as well as coverings that hold conditioning chemicals tightly against one's hair.

SADDLE UP AND PUT SPURS ON MY AIR FORCES

LYRIC FROM SONG: "MIDWEST SWING"   ON ALBUM: FREE CITY   BY ARTIST: ST. LUNATICS

A specific style of Nike tennis shoes could in theory be fitted with an accessory worn by cowboys to encourage movement in horses. This idea helps illustrate that I have not gotten caught up in the excitement of the East Coast or West Coast and associated big-city lifestyles the residents thereof take pride in, and can instead enjoy the conveniences of an urban environment with easy access to the country freedom associated with cities in the Midwest.

CAN'T WEAR SKINNY JEANS 'CAUSE MY KNOTS DON'T FIT

LYRIC FROM SONG: **"SWAGGA LIKE US"** ON ALBUM: **PAPER TRAIL** BY ARTIST: **T.I.**

I am unable to wear tight-fitting denim bottoms that are currently fashionable among some groups of people, so instead I wear arguably more fashionable and definitely more loose-fitting Rocawear brand trousers because the items contained within require the extra room they provide.

4X, YOU CAN'T SEE THE SEMIAUTOMATIC

LYRIC FROM SONG: **"THROW BACK"** ON ALBUM: **STREET DREAMS** BY ARTIST: **FABOLOUS**

When one wears an oversized top, such as a throwback jersey featuring a sports team logo from years ago, they are able to better conceal weapons that might be hidden in the waist of their trousers.

GETTIN' UNRELEASED JORDANS STRAIGHT FROM TOKYO

LYRIC FROM SONG: **"DEM BOYZ"**   ON ALBUM: **U GOTTA FEEL ME**   BY ARTIST: **LIL' FLIP**

It is desirable to have the newest popular fashions as soon as, or in some cases before, they are released to the public, and sneakers worn and marketed by one of the greatest basketball players of all time might conceivably be procured in a large city in Asia, where they might be sold before they are shipped to the United States.

HOCKEY PLAYERS PAGIN' ME TO PRACTICE ON MY WRIST

LYRIC FROM SONG: **"ICE-E"**   ON ALBUM: **WHO'S THE BOSS**
BY ARTIST: **NELLY & THE ST. LUNATICS**

I have so much diamond jewelry covering the end of my arm near my hand that individuals who enjoy a certain cold-weather contact sport are contacting me on my outdated alphanumeric communication device, having confused my bracelet for an ice rink they would like to use to improve their athletic abilities.

MY DIAMONDS, MY FITTED, AND MY MINK ON

LYRIC FROM SONG: "JUST A LIL BIT"   ON ALBUM: **THE MASSACRE**   BY ARTIST: **50 CENT**

I like my attire to consist of crystals that were mined from beneath the earth's surface, a head covering that conforms perfectly to the size of my crown without requiring an unsightly plastic adjustment strap, and the fur of a small forest-dwelling weasel-like creature that provides both comfort and warmth.

SHE GOT ON PAYLESS; ME, I GOT ON GATOR SHOES

LYRIC FROM SONG: **"P.I.M.P."** ON ALBUM: **GET RICH OR DIE TRYIN'** BY ARTIST: **50 CENT**

The woman I am associating with has covered her feet with items purchased from a retail chain that is known for emphasizing value over excess and, in contrast, I am wearing much more expensive foot coverings made from the skin of a reptile native to the south-eastern United States. Although this doesn't necessarily prevent me from associating with her, it is indicative of our different positions on an economic scale.

SKILLS
AND
PRIDE

BEEN A PLAYER SINCE FREEZE POPS

LYRIC FROM SONG: **"SCANDALOUS"**   ON ALBUM: **FREE CITY**   BY ARTIST: **ST. LUNATICS**

During my youth, I began exhibiting qualities associated with one who excels at convincing women to concede to his own selfish sexual interests, and this happened at the same approximate time that I began consuming frozen fruit-flavored treats packaged in plastic tubes.

GETTIN' FUNKY ON THE MIKE LIKE A OLD BATCH O' COLLARD GREENS

LYRIC FROM SONG: **"NUTHIN' BUT A 'G' THANG"**   ON ALBUM: **THE CHRONIC**   BY ARTIST: **DR. DRE**

Because they both cause people to take notice, someone rapping in a skillful manner is compared to an odiferous quantity of leafy plants that have been cooked and have been sitting at room temperature for quite some time.

FLOW SO COLD, CHICKEN SOUP WON'T HELP

LYRIC FROM SONG: **"LOLLIPOP (REMIX)"**   ON ALBUM: **THA CARTER III (ITUNES BONUS TRACK)**
BY ARTIST: **LIL WAYNE**

The stream of lyrics that travels from my mouth to the microphone is so powerful that if it were a treatable sickness, a common home remedy would have no effect.

BEEN SMOOTH SINCE DAYS OF UNDEROOS

LYRIC FROM SONG: **"HYPNOTIZE"** ON ALBUM: **LIFE AFTER DEATH**
BY ARTIST: **THE NOTORIOUS B.I.G.**

I never experienced any of the awkward or clumsy moments many individuals suffer through in their youth. Rather, I have been able to carry myself with a confidence that has resulted in the handling of situations with unfaltering ease ever since I wore a certain brand of children's underpants featuring cartoon, comic, and movie characters.

GOT THE TITLE FROM MY MAMA, PUT THE WHIP IN MY OWN NAME NOW

LYRIC FROM SONG: **"RIDE WIT ME"** ON ALBUM: **COUNTRY GRAMMAR** BY ARTIST: **NELLY**

I obtained from my mother the document that proves ownership of a vehicle that I have been driving. There may have been an arrangement for this document to previously reflect her as owner either because of my poor credit or in order to keep the vehicle in the family should I run into legal trouble and it otherwise be impounded by law enforcement. Regardless of the reason, and now that I have established a high level of monetary success, I will take this document and full responsibility for the vehicle.

I AIN'T PASS THE BAR, BUT I KNOW A LITTLE BIT

LYRIC FROM SONG: **"99 PROBLEMS"** ON ALBUM: **THE BLACK ALBUM** BY ARTIST: **JAY-Z**

Although I haven't educated myself concerning all the matters necessary to complete the examination lawyers take to be able to practice law, I have enough knowledge about legal issues to know when someone is violating my rights.

NOW MY GRANDMAMA AIN'T THE ONLY GIRL CALLIN' ME BABY

LYRIC FROM SONG: **"GOOD LIFE"** ON ALBUM: **GRADUATION** BY ARTIST: **KANYE WEST**

During my youth, my parent's mother called me "baby" as a way to show me I was loved. Now that I am successful, females who are not members of my family call me by that same name in a romantic way.

STUNTIN' IS A HABIT

LYRIC FROM SONG: **"GET LIKE ME"**   ON ALBUM: **THE GREATEST STORY EVER TOLD**
BY ARTIST: **DAVID BANNER**

Engaging in showy behavior that brings me as much attention as
a stuntman would receive from an audience observing his death-
defying maneuver is something I do on a regular basis without
taking much notice of or making it a point to emphasize.

HOPPED UP OUT THE BED, TURNED MY SWAG ON

LYRIC FROM SONG: **"TURN MY SWAG ON"**   ON ALBUM: **ISOULJABOYTELLEM**
BY ARTIST: **SOULJA BOY TELL 'EM**

I anxiously approach a new day by leaping from my place of slumber,
and I immediately establish a mind-set of confidence, success, and
pride, which can be sensed from the way I walk, talk, and act.

CAN'T STOP 'TIL I SEE MY NAME ON A BLIMP

LYRIC FROM SONG: **"MO MONEY MO PROBLEMS"** ON ALBUM: **LIFE AFTER DEATH** BY ARTIST: **THE NOTORIOUS B.I.G.**

I have to keep rapping and engaging in lucrative and successful business practices until I have achieved one of my dreams: to have my name displayed in lights on the exterior of a dirigible.

I WAS A O.G. IN THE HOOD BEFORE I TURNED TWENTY-TWO

LYRIC FROM SONG: **"WESTSIDE STORY"** ON ALBUM: **THE DOCUMENTARY** BY ARTIST: **THE GAME**

At a young age, I was considered an original gangster, a term usually reserved for someone who has engaged in the same type of behavior as me for a very long period and has gradually established their reputation. I was rapidly promoted to this level of respect due to the large amount of gangsterlike activity I engaged in within a relatively short time.

SO MUCH DIRT, I NEED TO BE IN THE *GUINNESS BOOK*

LYRIC FROM SONG: **"AMERIKKKA'S MOST WANTED"**   ON ALBUM: **AMERIKKKA'S MOST WANTED**
BY ARTIST: **ICE CUBE**

So many things have taken place of an unclean nature that a new category for such a thing should be created for me in a well-known record book.

NEVER KNOWN AS A SWEATER

LYRIC FROM SONG: **"2 LEGIT 2 QUIT"**   ON ALBUM: **TOO LEGIT TO QUIT**
BY ARTIST: **MC HAMMER**

Nobody who is associated with me would ever expect that I would act nervously when confronted with a difficult situation because I am known as a cool individual who can handle anything that comes my way without perspiring.

I CALL ALL THE SHOTS, RIP ALL THE SPOTS, ROCK ALL THE ROCKS, COP ALL THE DROPS

LYRIC FROM SONG: **"MO MONEY MO PROBLEMS"**   ON ALBUM: **LIFE AFTER DEATH**
BY ARTIST: **THE NOTORIOUS B.I.G.**

I tell everyone what to do or make all the decisions, I have a good time going to all the popular locations, I wear all the best diamond jewelry, and I obtain all the convertible vehicles.

HATED ON SO MUCH, *PASSION OF CHRIST* NEED A SEQUEL

LYRIC FROM SONG: **"MY LIFE"** ON ALBUM: **LAX** BY ARTIST: **THE GAME**

I have been unjustly persecuted for my actions and the things I have said to the point that were a movie to be made of my life, it could be marketed as a follow-up to a popular film about the life and death of Jesus.

I DON'T JUST RHYME, I OWN LIQUOR STORES AND SUCH

LYRIC FROM SONG: **"SPORTS, DRUGS & ENTERTAINMENT"** ON ALBUM: **S.D.E.**
BY ARTIST: **CAM'RON**

Not only do I provide myself with income as a successful rapper, but I am also involved in various business ventures or investment opportunities, such as the purchase of highly profitable shops that sell alcohol.

THE WAY I FLOSS, Y'ALL CHICKENS SHOULD BE CLUCKIN'

LYRIC FROM SONG: **"ALL THE CHICKENS"** ON ALBUM: **S.D.E.** BY ARTIST: **CAM'RON**

My appearance, highlighted by my stylish clothes, fancy car, and expensive jewelry, which is so clean that the only thing left for me to do would seem to be to put the finishing touches on my teeth with a piece of string, should make women who I treat like domesticated poultry provide sexually for me.

YOU SAY THE LIQUOR STORE, I SAY BRINKS

LYRIC FROM SONG: **"FORCED TO DO DIRT"**　ON ALBUM: **VI—RETURN OF THE REAL**
BY ARTIST: **ICE T**

I have set much more ambitious goals than you when it comes to acquiring wealth, with your focus on trivial amounts, such as those contained within the cash register at a somewhat low-security alcoholic beverage retailer, and my focus on the much larger quantities contained within an armored vehicle operated by a private currency transport company.

I DROP UNEXPECTEDLY, LIKE BIRD SHIT

LYRIC FROM SONG: **"KICK IN THE DOOR"**　ON ALBUM: **LIFE AFTER DEATH**
BY ARTIST: **THE NOTORIOUS B.I.G.**

Just as many people are not aware of winged animals' cloacal expulsions until they are actually defecated upon, nobody expects to hear the amazing lyrics I utter while rapping, and they are shocked and impressed.

NO MORE HATERS, NO BLOWIN' NINTENDO CARTRIDGES

LYRIC FROM SONG: **"DIAMOND IN THE BACK"** ON ALBUM: **CHICKEN -N- BEER**
BY ARTIST: **LUDACRIS**

Now that I am successful I no longer have to worry about the annoyances of life, such as people who disrespect me or having to forcefully exhale into a video game to displace dust that may have been preventing an electrical connection to be made to a popular video game console.

PEOPLE

I'M DOIN' THE HULK HOGAN, BUT THEY AIN'T SAYIN' NOTHIN'

LYRIC FROM SONG: **"AIN'T SAYIN' NOTHIN' (REMIX)"** BY ARTIST: **FAT JOE**

I am mimicking the motion of a professional wrestler in which he spins his hand around a few times before holding it behind his ear to encourage the crowd to cheer more loudly. I am using this motion to see if people have anything bad to say about me, but they are afraid to speak.

THOUGHT I WAS BURNT UP LIKE PEPSI DID MICHAEL

LYRIC FROM SONG: "THROUGH THE WIRE"   ON ALBUM: **THE COLLEGE DROPOUT**
BY ARTIST: **KANYE WEST**

When I got in a serious car accident, my adoring fans feared the worst, thinking I had sustained serious burns to my body like Michael Jackson did while on the set of a Pepsi commercial he was filming during the 1980s.

CALL ME GEORGE FOREMAN 'CAUSE I'M SELLIN' EVERYBODY GRILLZ

LYRIC FROM SONG: **"GRILLZ"** ON ALBUM: **SWEATSUIT** BY ARTIST: **NELLY**

I am receiving money in exchange for the decorative gold-and-diamond-studded mouthpieces people in the community are wearing, and my popularity is similar to that a former boxer had while successfully selling convenient food-cooking appliances.

TOP GUN SHUT DOWN YOUR FIRM LIKE TOM CRUISE

LYRIC FROM SONG: **"WOO HAH! GOT YOU ALL IN CHECK"** ON ALBUM: **THE COMING** BY ARTIST: **BUSTA RHYMES**

I am an expert rapper whose skills include the ability to reference two popular movies by the same actor in one line while at the same time delivering an insult to you and your group of friends, which highlights myself as someone with the confidence of a fighter pilot and you as hopeless as a corrupt group of lawyers facing prosecution.

I GOT GAME LIKE STUART SCOTT

LYRIC FROM SONG: **"3 PEAT"**   ON ALBUM: **THA CARTER III**   BY ARTIST: **LIL WAYNE**

My skills pursuing and attracting women are on par with the great familiarity a knowledgeable reporter displays while hosting a television program summarizing recent sporting events.

PEOPLE HATE ME LIKE BILL O'REILLY

LYRIC FROM SONG: **"TRUNK BANG"**   ON ALBUM: **DORROUGH MUSIC**   BY ARTIST: **DORROUGH**

People's jealousy of me because of my success is comparable to some people's intense dislike of an opinionated conservative talk show host who was previously involved in a feud with rapper Ludacris.

MY SWAGGER IS MICK JAGGER

LYRIC FROM SONG: **"SWAGGA LIKE US"** ON ALBUM: **PAPER TRAIL** BY ARTIST: **T.I.**

My assured attitude and corresponding body language matches that of the Rolling Stones singer and front man who is known for his confident strut on the stage.

HE 'BOUT TO GO OUT LIKE SCARFACE

LYRIC FROM SONG: **"THUG ANGELS"**   ON ALBUM: **THE ECLEFTIC: 2 SIDES II A BOOK**
BY ARTIST: **WYCLEF JEAN**

A person is about to leave this earth with the same conviction that character Tony Montana, a Cuban gangster in a movie about the rise to power of a cocaine dealer that is loved by much of the rap community, had while putting up a strong fight with an automatic weapon in an attempt to defend himself and his home and business even though he was outnumbered.

THE RING I GOT, LIBERACE WANT IT

LYRIC FROM SONG: **"FLOSSIN' SEASON"**   ON ALBUM: **400 DEGREEZ**   BY ARTIST: **JUVENILE**

The band on my finger is of such great value that a certain very wealthy and flamboyant pianist with a penchant for extravagant clothing and jewelry and who was known for somewhat frivolous purchases of such items would have liked to have had it in his collection.

AL ROKER, I USED TO KNOCK POUNDS OFF

LYRIC FROM SONG: **"HATE"**   ON ALBUM: **THE BLUEPRINT 3**   BY ARTIST: **JAY-Z**

A weatherman from television lost weight through surgery, diet, and exercise, while I got rid of large quantities of drugs in an undisclosed manner.

I'M ABOUT TO GET MY BILL CLINTON ON

LYRIC FROM SONG: **"EVERYGIRL IN THE WORLD"** ON ALBUM: **WE ARE YOUNG MONEY**
BY ARTIST: **YOUNG MONEY**

I am about to receive oral sex from a woman I am in a position of power over and then possibly state that I have not had sexual relations with her if anyone asks.

I GOT MORE RHYMES THAN CARL SAGAN'S GOT TURTLENECKS

LYRIC FROM SONG: **"HEY FUCK YOU"**   ON ALBUM: **TO THE 5 BOROUGHS**
BY ARTIST: **BEASTIE BOYS**

The number of rap lyrics I have recited is greater than the number of sweaters contained in a famous astrophysicist's wardrobe.

GAVE BILL GATES SOME BINOCULARS AND SAID LOOK OUT FOR ME

LYRIC FROM SONG: **"ON TOP OF THE WORLD"** ON ALBUM: **PAPER TRAIL** BY ARTIST: **T.I.**

Were wealth measured by distance and because I may soon be surpassing one of the richest men in the world in net worth, he would require a pair of small, handheld telescopes in addition to his corrective lenses to see me.

BOTTLE-SHAPED BODY LIKE MRS. BUTTERWORTH

LYRIC FROM SONG: "TOUCH THE SKY"   ON ALBUM: LATE REGISTRATION
BY ARTIST: **KANYE WEST**

Your curvaceous figure, highlighted by your breasts and hips, resembles the shape of a pancake syrup container that looks like a woman some people find attractive.

I'M GANGSTA— MORE LIKE DEEBO WHEN HE WAS ZEUS

LYRIC FROM SONG: "WESTSIDE STORY"   ON ALBUM: THE DOCUMENTARY   BY ARTIST: **THE GAME**

I'm less like the character that actor Tom Lister Jr. played in the movie *Friday*, who was somewhat dumb, and more like the character he played opposite Hulk Hogan in the movie *No Holds Barred*, who was very strong and difficult to harm.

JAMES BOND, JACKIE CHAN, AND THAT BITCH MACGYVER

LYRIC FROM SONG: **"#1 STUNNA"** ON ALBUM: **I GOT THAT WORK** BY ARTIST: **BIG TYMERS**

The items I own and the behavior I engage in are as impressive and awe-inspiring as those of a spy from books and movies, a famous martial artist who showcases his skills in films, and the main character from a television show of the same name who uses his mental abilities and readily available objects to get himself and others out of difficult situations.

SHOW YOU HOW TO WILD OUT LIKE JACK TRIPPER

LYRIC FROM SONG: **"SO FRESH, SO CLEAN"** ON ALBUM: **STANKONIA** BY ARTIST: **OUTKAST**

I will demonstrate behavior you can mimic should you want to have as fun and crazy a time as a mistakenly homosexual character from a television show that began in the 1970s who lived with two women and often had a difficult time staying calm.

FLOW RETARDED SORTA LIKE THAT RAIN MAN

LYRIC FROM SONG: **"SAY YEAH"** BY ARTIST: **WIZ KHALIFA**

My rapping ability is so shocking in its effectiveness that listeners feel stunned when they hear me and I therefore compare my abilities to those of a movie character who was an autistic savant and may at times have caused people that observed him to become speechless.

IF JEEZY'S PAYIN' LEBRON, I'M PAYIN' DWYANE WADE

LYRIC FROM SONG: **"EMPIRE STATE OF MIND"** ON ALBUM: **THE BLUEPRINT 3** BY ARTIST: **JAY-Z**

Were another successful rapper to pay the budget price of $23,000 for a certain large quantity of a particular drug, which happens to reflect one basketball player's jersey number multiplied by 1,000, I might be able to procure the same quantity of that drug for only $3,000, which is an amount equal to a different basketball player's jersey multiplied by 1,000 and an excellent bargain.

NINO COULDN'T DO IT, BUT THEN WAYNE HIT THA CARTER

LYRIC FROM SONG: **"UPS AND DOWNS"** ON ALBUM: **BACK ON MY BUCK SHIT**
BY ARTIST: **YOUNG BUCK**

In the 1991 movie *New Jack City*, Wesley Snipes plays a character named Nino Brown, who takes over an apartment complex called the Carter but has to give up his drug business there. In contrast, rapper Lil Wayne gained fortune and fame through the release of his album *Tha Carter*, which he continues to enjoy today.

PLACES

CREEP TO THE PAD 'CAUSE MOM'S GOT THE GRUB ON THE GRILL

LYRIC FROM SONG: **"1ST OF THA MONTH"**   ON ALBUM: **E 1999 ETERNAL**
BY ARTIST: **BONE THUGS-N-HARMONY**

Slowly make our way by car or sneak by foot to Mother's house because she is cooking dinner and she will surely let us partake in the meal, which will energize us for the rest of the night's activities.

LIKE MCDONALD'S, I WAS FLIPPIN' THEM ORDERS

LYRIC FROM SONG: "MONEY" ON ALBUM: LAX BY ARTIST: THE GAME

One may be so good at taking people's requests for drugs, receiving their money, and providing them with the product they requested in a timely manner that one rivals the admirable speed with which a major fast-food chain provides its patrons with delicious hamburgers and French fries.

AFTER THE PARTY IT'S THE HOTEL LOBBY

LYRIC FROM SONG: "IGNITION (REMIX)" ON ALBUM: CHOCOLATE FACTORY BY ARTIST: R. KELLY

The sequence of events that happens following a celebratory gathering is that we congregate in the front room immediately inside the entrance to our temporary lodging to mingle before pairing up and making our way to more private quarters to get to know each other better.

I'VE GOT HOES IN DIFFERENT AREA CODES

LYRIC FROM SONG: **"AREA CODES"** ON ALBUM: **WORD OF MOUF** BY ARTIST: **LUDACRIS**

I have females in various parts of the United States who are represented by the three digits that begin the telephone numbers allocated for the regions in which they reside, providing me with many possibilities for companionship as I travel the world, should I care to contact them.

BODIES BEIN' FOUND ON GREENLEAF

LYRIC FROM SONG: **"LET ME RIDE"** ON ALBUM: **THE CHRONIC** BY ARTIST: **DR. DRE**

At one point in time, a major boulevard in Compton near Los Angeles was a dumping ground where bodies were often placed following murders, so it would be possible to happen upon a cadaver if you frequent this area.

CLAIMIN' DETROIT WHEN Y'ALL LIVE TWENTY MILES AWAY

LYRIC FROM SONG: **"MARSHALL MATHERS"**   ON ALBUM: **THE MARSHALL MATHERS LP** BY ARTIST: **EMINEM**

You tell people you live within the city of Detroit, which contains many rough neighborhoods, but in fact you have never experienced true urban life because in reality you live in the safety of the suburbs outside the city limits.

THEY EVEN MADE ME SHOW ID TO GET INSIDE OF SAM'S CLUB

LYRIC FROM SONG: **"NEVER LET ME DOWN"**   ON ALBUM: **THE COLLEGE DROPOUT**
BY ARTIST: **KANYE WEST**

I was required to show proof of who I was before being permitted to enter a warehouse store where security is not known to be particularly tight, and this may have happened because of racism.

ROCKS AND PRESIDENTS LIKE MOUNT RUSHMORE

LYRIC FROM SONG: **"MONEY"**   ON ALBUM: **LAX**   BY ARTIST: **THE GAME**

When seen together, crack cocaine pieces and paper currency showing the faces of former U.S. leaders might remind one of the sculpted mountains at a national landmark in the state of South Dakota.

ONE OF US GONNA SEE THE CEMETERY

LYRIC FROM SONG: **"HOW DO U WANT IT"**   ON ALBUM: **ALL EYEZ ON ME**   BY ARTIST: **2PAC**

We are very angry with each other and refuse to concede anything in an argument. Therefore, one of us may visit a neighborhood burial area for a permanent stay.

BIG PIMPIN' DOWN IN P-A-T

LYRIC FROM SONG: **"BIG PIMPIN'"** ON ALBUM: **VOL. 3: LIFE AND TIMES OF S. CARTER**
BY ARTIST: **JAY-Z**

We are engaging in celebratory activities in Port Arthur, Texas, that are similar to those the manager of a group of prostitutes may partake in, but done on a much larger scale.

SO MUCH DRAMA IN THE L-B-C

LYRIC FROM SONG: **"GIN AND JUICE"**   ON ALBUM: **DOGGYSTYLE**
BY ARTIST: **SNOOP DOGGY DOGG**

There are so many wild and unbelievable things happening in Long Beach, California, on a regular basis that it is difficult for me to wrap my head around them, let alone explain them to you in a three-minute song.

SWAP MEETS, STICKY GREEN, AND BAD TRAFFIC

LYRIC FROM SONG: **"STILL D.R.E."** ON ALBUM: **2001** BY ARTIST: **DR. DRE**

Three things that I strongly associate with the city of Los Angeles, California, or the particular neighborhood within which I live, are frequent gatherings where people buy, sell, and trade goods; marijuana of a particular texture and color; and congested roadways.

SLANG ON THE DOUBLE NINE

LYRIC FROM SONG: **"1ST OF THA MONTH"** ON ALBUM: **E 1999 ETERNAL**
BY ARTIST: **BONE THUGS-N-HARMONY**

Illegal drugs are sold on E. 99th Street south of Interstate 90 in the northeastern part of the city of Cleveland, Ohio.

HIT LAKE SHORE, GIRLS GO ALL CRAZY

LYRIC FROM SONG: **"DRIVE SLOW"**   ON ALBUM: **LATE REGISTRATION**
BY ARTIST: **KANYE WEST**

When we arrive at a major expressway along the eastern border of the city of Chicago, Illinois, that runs along the western coast of Lake Michigan, females become excited to see us and our nice cars.

I'M FROM THE LOU AND I'M PROUD

LYRIC FROM SONG: **"COUNTRY GRAMMAR"**   ON ALBUM: **COUNTRY GRAMMAR**   BY ARTIST: **NELLY**

I am not embarrassed to claim to be from the city of St. Louis, Missouri, in the midwestern United States, even though you may think a person who is a rapper would most like to be associated with the East or West Coast.

PEOPLE WANNA CRUISE CRENSHAW ON SUNDAY

LYRIC FROM SONG: **"I WISH"** ON ALBUM: **I WISH** BY ARTIST: **SKEE-LO**

Some like to aimlessly drive in their cars back and forth on a major boulevard in the city of Los Angeles, California, to speak out the car window to friends, play their stereo systems, show off their cars, and wind down the weekend before going back to work on Monday.

ATL HOE, DON'T DISRESPECT IT

LYRIC FROM SONG: **"GET LOW"** ON ALBUM: **KINGS OF CRUNK**
BY ARTIST: **LIL JON & THE EAST SIDE BOYZ**

I will call you a name as a form of persuasion to prevent you from thinking or saying bad things about the city of Atlanta, Georgia, because it is a city I am proud of.

I'M FROM THE BAY, WHERE WE HYPHY AND GO DUMB

LYRIC FROM SONG: **"TELL ME WHEN TO GO"** ON ALBUM: **MY GHETTO REPORT CARD**
BY ARTIST: **E-40**

I am from the Oakland/San Francisco, California, area, which is a location where people engage in hyperactive behavior and possibly foolish yet amusing and fun activities without regard to their appearance and for the sake of enjoyment.

WENT TO JACOB AN HOUR AFTER I GOT MY ADVANCE

LYRIC FROM SONG: **"TOUCH THE SKY"**   ON ALBUM: **LATE REGISTRATION**
BY ARTIST: **KANYE WEST**

Shortly after I signed a deal with a record company, I made my way to a shop owned by Jacob the Jeweler, who outfits celebrities and sports stars with expensive fashion accessories, because I am now able to afford such things after receiving money in exchange for future record sales.

I REP THE DIRTY DIRTY WHERE THEY MOVE 'CAINE

LYRIC FROM SONG: **"TURN IT UP"** ON ALBUM: **THE SOUND OF REVENGE**
BY ARTIST: **CHAMILLIONAIRE**

I am an ambassador from an area in the southern United States referred to as the Dirty South, and this is a place where cocaine is received, trafficked, and sold, because it is one of the shorter routes by sea from South America to the continental United States.

ACKNOWLEDGMENTS

I'D LIKE TO THANK R. A. Montgomery and Edward Packard for making reading books enjoyable; the producers of the television show *In Living Color* for initially exposing me to rap music; MC Hammer for putting his heart into *Too Legit to Quit*; Pro Set for releasing *Yo! MTV Raps* trading cards; Michael Nankin and David Wechter for the movie *Midnight Madness*; Chris, Ryan, and Craig from wE=MCs² for some inspirational studio and freestyle sessions; everyone who ever helped me with, contributed to, or visited UnderstandRap.com for their support; Abrams books for believing in and publishing this book; my friend Jon for convincing me it would be a good idea to spend a couple hours in the spring of 1998 watching the movie *House Party* and writing down every slang term we heard and didn't understand; Tom, John, and Dan for being great friends and helping to shape my sense of humor; Mom and Dad for their unconditional love and support; and my Lord and Savior, Jesus Christ.